Mysteries

Monica Hughes

Nelson

Contents

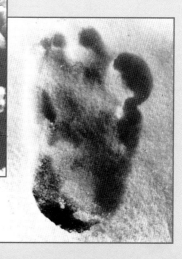

Introduction

A mystery is something that is strange and hard to understand.

This book is about some mysteries. They are shown on this map of the world.

Have you heard of some of these mysteries?

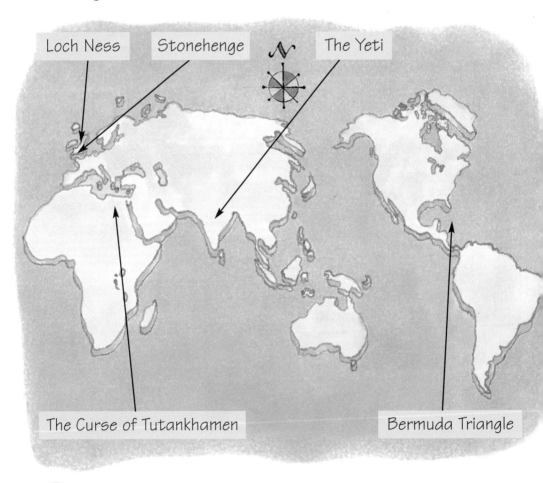

Loch Ness
Stonehenge
The Yeti
The Curse of Tutankhamen
Bermuda Triangle

The Loch Ness Monster

In Scotland, there is a lake called Loch Ness. This lake is big and deep.

There has been a mystery about this lake for many years.

Some people think a strange monster lives in the lake.

They say they have seen a monster with a long neck and a little head.

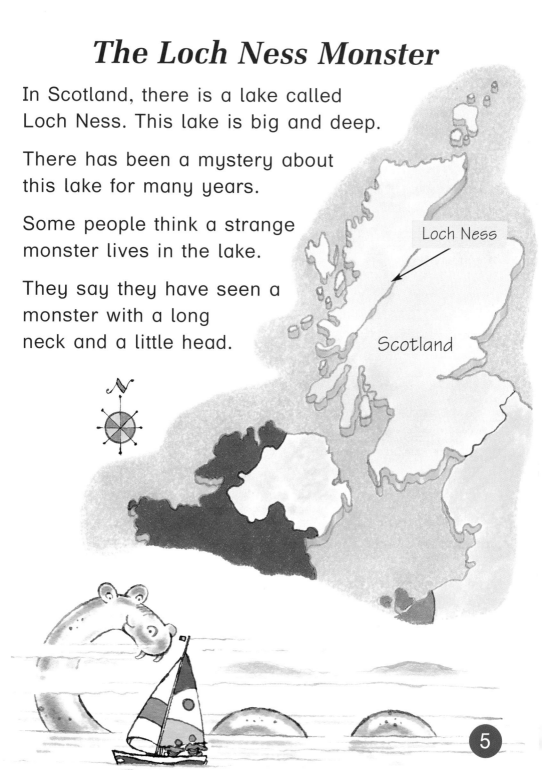

Loch Ness

Scotland

Photographs and films of the lake seem to show a monster.

Lots of people think these photographs and films are fakes.

Scientists don't know if there really is a monster in the lake. For many years, they have looked in the lake. They have used boats with sonar equipment. They have also used divers.

No-one has found the monster.

Scientists agree that there is something in the lake.

They don't know what it is.

Stonehenge

There is not just one mystery about Stonehenge, but two.

- How was it built?

- Why was it built?

People once thought Stonehenge was built by giants or by a Wizard called Merlin.

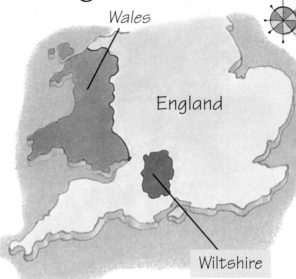

Wales

England

Wiltshire

Archaeologists now agree that it was started more than 4,000 years ago with stones from Wales.

Some of the stones are 6 metres tall and weigh 50 tonnes.

It is a mystery how people of long ago could move the stones all the way from Wales.

No-one knows why Stonehenge was built. Some people think it was a landing site for alien spaceships. It may have been an important meeting place. Maybe it is a stone calendar as it points to where the sun rises.

The Yeti

There are people
who think that a
strange animal lives
in the snow in the
Himalayan mountains.
They call it a Yeti or
'man-thing'.

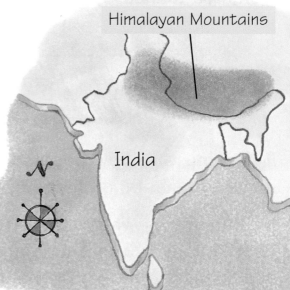

Some explorers have
seen strange tracks in
the snow. They have
taken photographs of
huge footprints. They
think the footprints
show an animal that
is about 3 metres tall
and weighs about
140 kilograms.

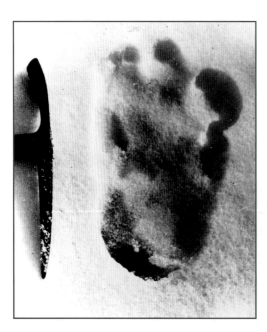

People say they have seen a Yeti. They say it looks like an ape and is covered in hair. They have heard loud screaming noises coming from the mountains, but is it a Yeti?

The Bermuda Triangle

There is a mystery about an area of sea off the coast of Florida, called the Bermuda Triangle.

More than two hundred ships and planes have disappeared in the Bermuda Triangle in the last one hundred years. Over one thousand people have also disappeared.

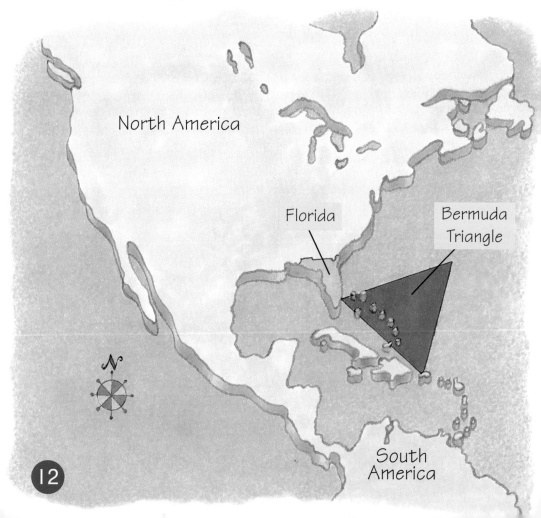

North America

Florida

Bermuda Triangle

N

South America

No-one knows what happens in the Bermuda Triangle. Scientists think the compasses on the ships and planes go wrong, and so accidents happen.

Some people think there is a strange whirlpool in the area. Other people think the Bermuda Triangle is the way into an alien world.

US Navy bomber planes disappeared in 1945.

The Marine Sulphur Queen disappeared on February 8th 1963.

The Curse of Tutankhamen

In 1922, an archaeologist called Howard Carter and his friend Lord Carnarvon found the tomb of King Tutankhamen, in Egypt.

The tomb was full of treasure. There was also a strange stone. The writing on the stone said there was a curse on anyone who went into the tomb.

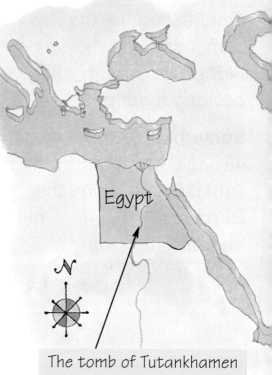

Egypt

The tomb of Tutankhamen

No-one knows if there was a curse, but Lord Carnarvon died the next year. Twenty-two other people who worked in the tomb died in the next four years.

Some people think there was poison in the tomb or a disease from long ago. The Egyptians who worked on the tomb didn't believe in the curse, and Howard Carter lived a long life.

Lord Carnarvon Claimed by Tutankhamen's Curse

Reuters, Cairo – Only five months after uncovering one of the most significant archaeological finds this century, Lord Carnarvon, patron of the excavations lead by Howard Carter, died yesterday of blood poisoning. Many here in Egypt believe that his death is a result of the curse placed on the tomb by high priests as part of burial rituals performed for royalty in Ancient Egyptian times.

Glossary

alien – a being from another world

archaeologist – someone who learns about the past by digging up old things

compass – an instrument with a needle that always points to the north

curse – to wish evil on someone

explorer – someone who travels to discover new things and places

fake – made to look like something real

mystery – something strange and hard to understand

sonar – the use of echo underwater to find things

whirlpool – water that is spinning very quickly

whirlwind – wind that is spinning very quickly

wizard – a man with magic power